MW00896754

Easy

Traditional

Duets

for

Two Flutes

28 traditional melodies from around the
world arranged for flute players. Starts
with the easiest.
Additional Christmas pieces.
All are in easy keys.

Amanda Oosthuizen

Jemima Oosthuizen

The Flying Flute Series

Wild Music Publications
www.wildmusicpublications.com

We hope you enjoy *Easy Traditional Duets for Two Flutes.*

Take a look at our other exciting books, including: Intermediate Classic Duets, 50+ Greatest Classics, Catch the Beat, Christmas Duets, Easy Tunes from Around the World, Trick or Treat – A Halloween Suite, Fish 'n' Ships, and more solo and duet books.

For more info on other amazing books, please go to:

WildMusicPublications.com

Visit our secret page for a **free backing track,** and more fun things for free! Go to:

http://WildMusicPublications.com/**2secret-flute2-tracks-42/**

And use the password: **FruityFlute27**

Happy Music Making!

The Wild Music Publications Team

To keep up –to-date with our new releases, why not **follow us on Twitter**

@WMPublications

Contents

THE SURPRISE

Start slowly and gradually inccrease speed

SPAIN

THIS LAND IS MY LAND

THE OLD TREE

Very slowly and solidly   GERMANY

THE VOLGA BOATMAN

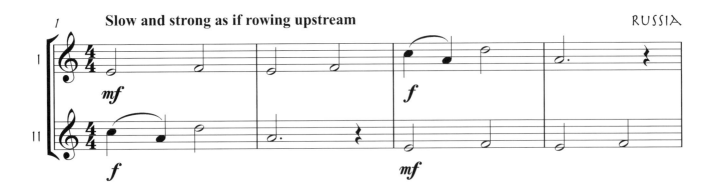

Slow and strong as if rowing upstream   RUSSIA

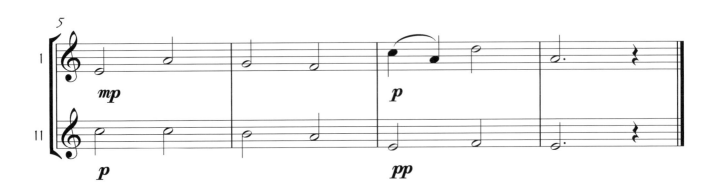

BOAT ON TAI LAKE

CHINA

SLEEP, SLEEP

LA BERGAMASCA

YANKEE DOODLE

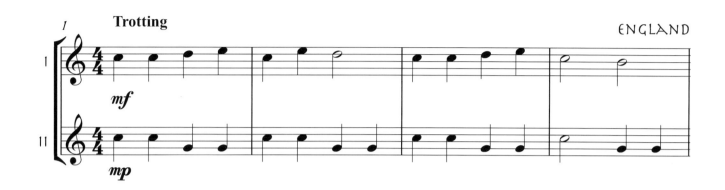

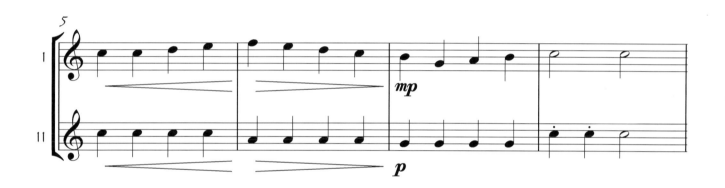

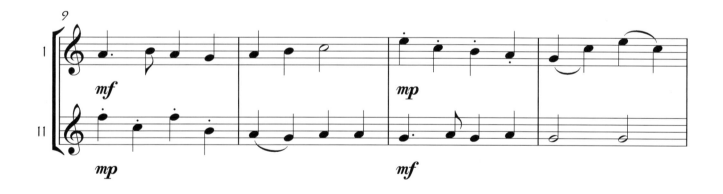

CLOWN'S DANCE

FRANCE

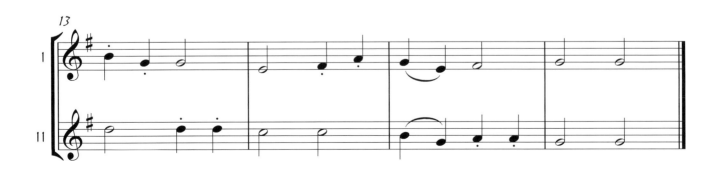

AWAY IN A MANGER

Gently rocking

TRADITIONAL

GIANTS

Heavily as if stamping

SWEDEN

THE COBBLER

CZECH REPUBLIC

Heavily as if hammering

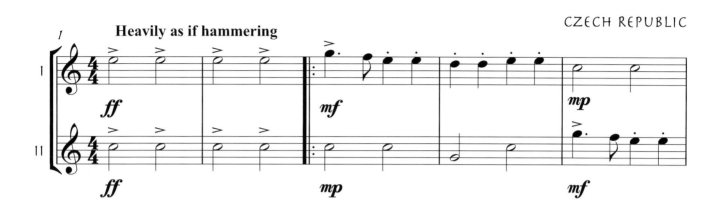

THE WINDMILL

ENGLAND

MARIA

U.S.A.

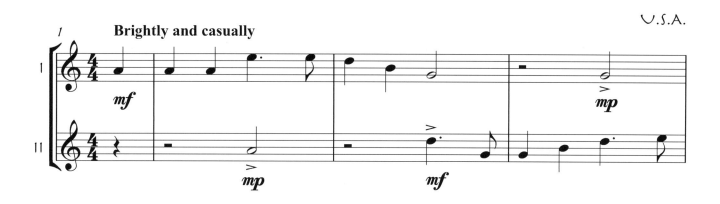

OLD MAN OF THE WOODS

WALES

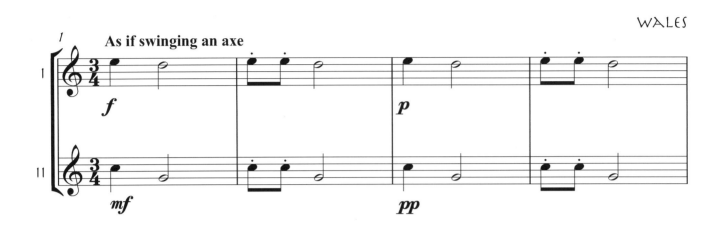

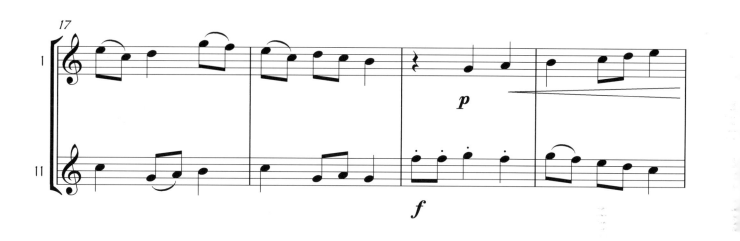

KOOKABURRA

AUSTRALIA

CRIPPLE CREEK

U.S.A.

J'AI UN BON TABAC

FRANCE

LIGHTLY ROW

As if rowing but not fast

GERMANY

WE THREE KINGS

Not too fast as if riding a camel

TRADITIONAL

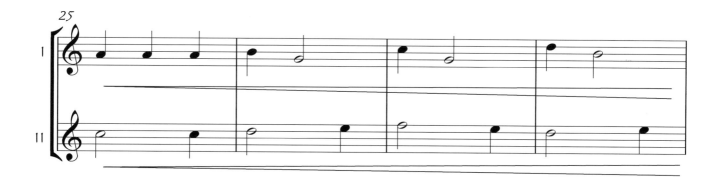

HEY HO, ANYBODY HOME?

U.S.A.

Happily as if knocking at a door

WILL THE CIRCLE BE UNBROKEN

Thoughtfully and not too fast

U.S.A.

WE WISH YOU A MERRY CHRISTMAS

TRADITIONAL

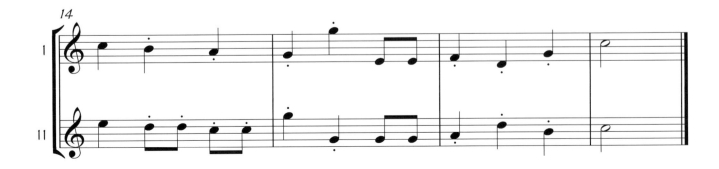

MOLLY MALONE

IRELAND

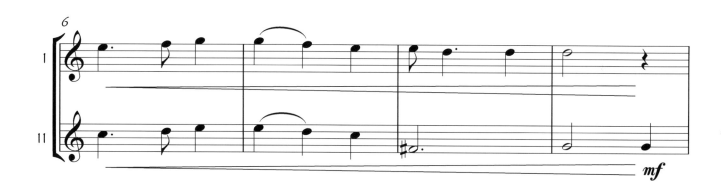

SWEET BETSY FROM PIKE

Lively and springing

U.S.A.

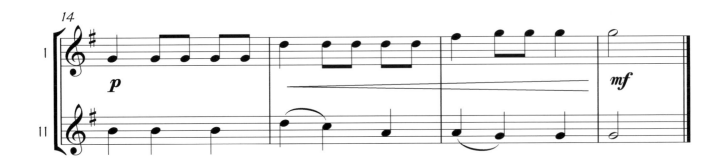

DECK THE HALLS

Lively and cheerfully

WALES

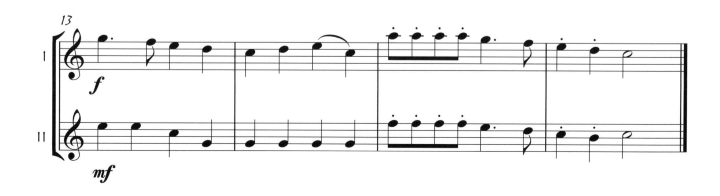

O MY DARLING CLEMENTINE

U.S.A.

MATILDA

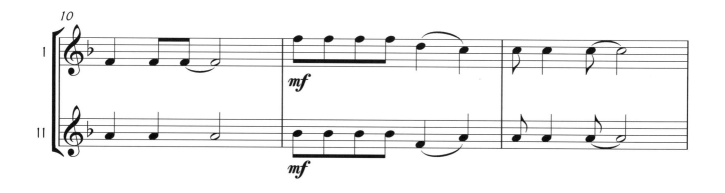

SILENT NIGHT

SUR LE PONT D'AVIGNON

FRANCE

JINGLE BELLS

BOBBY SHAFTOE

ENGLAND

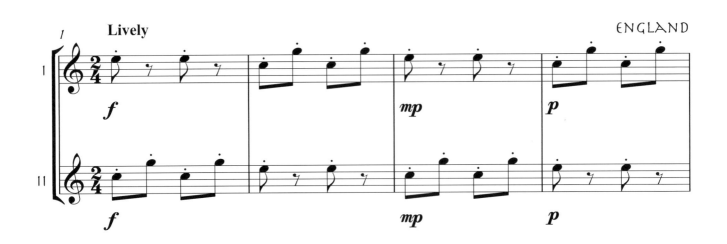

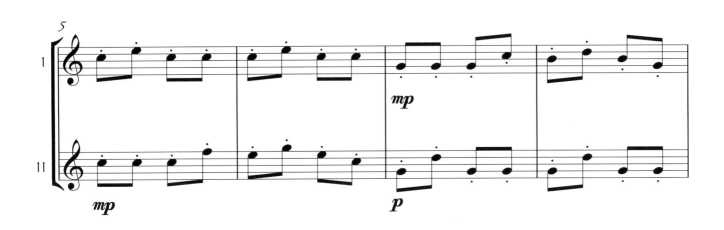

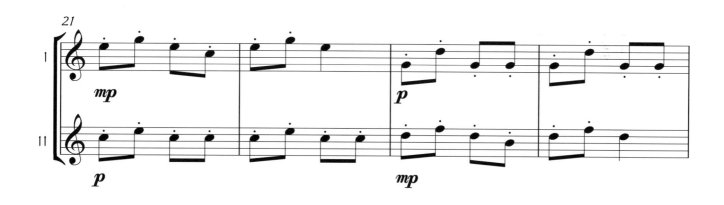

If you have enjoyed **Easy Traditional Duets for Two Flutes,** why not try the other books in the **Flying Flute Series**!

For more info, please visit: **WildMusicPublications.com**

All of our books are available to download, or you can order from Amazon.

Introducing:

Christmas Duets

Intermediate Classic Duets

Easy Duets from Around the World

Moonlight and Roses

50+ Greatest Classics

Fish 'n' Ships

Christmas Carols

Champagne and Chocolate

Easy Tunes from Around the World

Made in the USA
Coppell, TX
15 September 2021